You Are My Sunshine

A Medley of Colorful Quilts for Kids

by Christiane Meunier & Karen Bates

CHITRA PUBLICATIONS

Your Best Value in Quilting

www.QuiltTownUSA.com

Chitra Publications
2 Public Avenue
Montrose, Pennsylvania 18801-1220

First Printing: 2002

Library of Congress Cataloging-in-Publication Data

Meunier, Christiane, 1952-
    You are my sunshine : a medley of colorful quilts for kids / by
    Christiane Meunier and Karen Bates.
        p. cm.
    ISBN 1-885588-46-1 (pbk.)
    1. Patchwork—Patterns. 2. Children's quilts. I Bates, Karen, 1954-
II. Title.
    TT835 .M48724 2002
    746.46'041—dc21

                                    2002007073

Edited by: Deborah Hearn and Virginia Jones
Design and Illustrations: Brenda Pytlik
Photography: Van Zandbergen Photography, Brackney, Pennsylvania
Cover Photography: Guy Cali Associates, Inc., Clarks Summit, Pennsylvania

Our Mission Statement:

*We publish quality quilting magazines and books
that recognize, promote, and inspire self-expression.
We are dedicated to serving our customers
with respect, kindness, and efficiency.*
www.QuiltTownUSA.com

Play songs and lullabies remind us of how a child finds pleasure in each new day. With that in mind, we made quilts with titles that anyone from age 2 to 102 will recognize. We know that with names like "Knick, Knack, Paddy Whack" and "Here We Go 'round the Mulberry Bush," you'll be dancing and singing as you make a quilt for that special child in your life.

As we designed these quilts, we kept in mind that busy mothers and grandmothers would appreciate time-saving methods. Using today's tools and techniques, we've made it child's play to stitch any one of these appealing quilts. No-template construction, used for most of the quilts presented here, allows you to spend time selecting favorite colors and fabrics. Choosing from the abundance of novelty prints at your local quilt shop will probably be the most difficult part of making any one of these delightful quilts.

Quilts like "Old McDonald Had a Farm," "Ring Around the Rosie," and "How Much Is That Doggie in the Window?" provide perfect places to showcase your child's favorite cartoon character or whimsical fairytale animal. Cut bright, colorful rectangles or triangles and frame them with fabric strips like those that surround jungle animals in "Playmate, Come Out and Play With Me" or characters from a much-loved book in "Do You Believe in Magic?". Create pinwheels in two sizes for "Rock-a-bye Baby," stars for "Twinkle, Twinkle Little Star," or circles for "I See the Moon and the Moon Sees Me." Or do the "Hokey Pokey" with bright Log Cabin-style blocks.

Even toddlers can help select a theme fabric. With appropriate supervision, older children might enjoy marking and fussy-cutting a few pieces for their quilt. No matter which quilt you choose to make, have fun passing on your love of quilting to a member of the next generation.

Christiane *Karen*

Publisher and author Christiane Meunier has been a leader in the quilt world for more than a decade, since she first introduced *Quilting Today* magazine. Her full-size and miniature quilts have appeared in that publication as well as in *Traditional Quiltworks* and *Miniature Quilts* magazines.

Karen Bates began quilting 20 years ago, just prior to the birth of her first child. The mother of four, she has had lots of experience making baby quilts! Along with her sister Julie Dock, she has co-authorized several books about quilting for children. Karen lives in Ashland, Oregon, with her children and the love of her life, Richard.

CONTENTS

Hokey Pokey

Make a bunch of little blocks and turn them all around, that's what it's all about!

Materials

- Assorted bright prints, each at least 6" square, and totaling at least 1 yard
- 2 yards white floral
- 1/2 yard bright pink
- 3 yards backing fabric
- 50" x 55" piece of batting

QUILT SIZE: 45 1/2" x 51"
BLOCK SIZE: 5 1/2" square

CUTTING

Dimensions include a 1/4" seam allowance. Cut the lengthwise white floral strips before cutting smaller pieces from that fabric.

- Cut 47: 1 1/2" x 1 3/4" rectangles, assorted bright prints
- Cut 47: 1 3/4" x 2 3/4" strips, assorted bright prints
- Cut 47: 1 3/4" x 3 3/4" strips, assorted bright prints
- Cut 47: 1 3/4" x 5" strips, assorted bright prints
- Cut 2: 3 1/2" x 52" lengthwise strips, white floral
- Cut 2: 3 1/2" x 42" lengthwise strips, white floral
- Cut 47: 1 1/2" squares, white floral
- Cut 47: 1 1/2" x 2 3/4" strips, white floral
- Cut 47: 1 1/2" x 3 3/4" strips, white floral
- Cut 47: 1 1/2" x 5" strips, white floral
- Cut 47: 1 1/2" x 6" strips, white floral
- Cut 3: 6" squares, white floral
- Cut 4: 6" x 11 1/2" rectangles, white floral
- Cut 1: 3 1/2" x 11" rectangle, white floral
- Cut 5: 2 1/2" x 44" strips, bright pink, for the binding

DIRECTIONS

- Stitch a 1 1/2" x 1 3/4" bright print strip to a 1 1/2" white floral square.

- Stitch a 1 3/4" x 2 3/4" bright print strip to the right side of the unit, as shown.
- Stitch a 1 1/2" x 2 3/4" white floral strip to the bottom of the unit.
- Continue adding strips in the same direction, stitching white floral strips to the bottom and left edges, and bright print strips to the top and right edges, as shown, to complete a block. Make 47. Set 2 aside for the border.

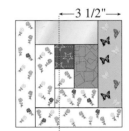

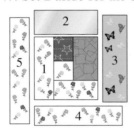

- Referring to the assembly diagram, lay out 45 blocks, the 6" white floral squares and the 6" x 11 1/2" white floral rectangles in 8 rows.
- Stitch the blocks, squares and rectangles into rows and join the rows.
- Trim the border blocks to 3 1/2" wide, as shown. Discard the light section of each trimmed block.

- Stitch a trimmed border block to the end of a 3 1/2" x 42" white floral strip, as shown.

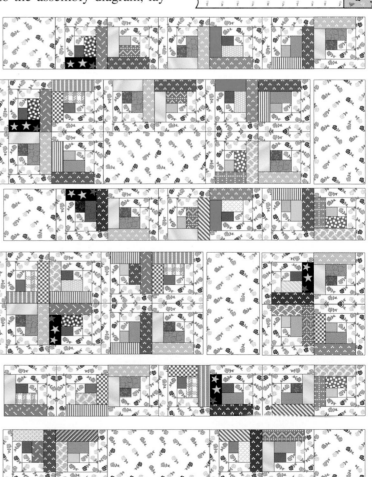

*Do the **"Hokey Pokey"** (45 1/2" x 51") and make this delightful quilt. Christiane is certain your child will enjoy following the multi-colored path that twists and turns across this fun design.*

• Measure the width of the quilt. Trim the pieced border to that measurement, removing the excess from the white floral end only. Stitch it to the top of the quilt.

• Trim the remaining 3 1/2" x 42" white floral strip to the measured width of the quilt and stitch it to the bottom of the quilt.

• Stitch a trimmed border block between a 3 1/2" x 11" white floral rectangle and a 3 1/2" x 52" white floral strip to make a pieced border, as shown.

• Pin the border to the left side of the quilt so that the bright fabrics in the border align with the bright trail in the quilt. Trim the excess from the ends of the border. Stitch the border to the quilt.

• Trim the remaining 3 1/2" x 52" white floral strip to the measured length of the quilt and stitch it to the right side of the quilt.

• Finish the quilt as described in the *General Directions*, using the 2 1/2" x 44" bright pink strips for the binding.

Playmate, Come Out and Play with Me

Make the most of jungle animal prints by simply framing cute motifs.

Materials

The yardage for the jungle print includes extra to allow for fussy-cutting the images.
- 1 yard jungle print
- 1 5/8 yards teal print
- 1/4 yard each of contrasting prints in red, dark purple, yellow, blue, and white
- 2 1/2 yards backing fabric
- 38" x 49" piece of batting
- Template plastic

QUILT SIZE: 34" x 45"
BLOCK SIZE: 10" square

CUTTING

Dimensions include a 1/4" seam allowance. Make a 3 1/2" square and a 3 1/2" x 8 1/2" see-through plastic template, and center animal motifs in each template when cutting fabric pieces. Cut the lengthwise teal print strips before cutting smaller pieces from that fabric.

For each of 12 blocks:
- Cut 2: 3 1/2" squares, jungle print
- Cut 1: 3 1/2" x 8 1/2" rectangle, jungle print. NOTE: *Half of the blocks require a horizontal image, and half require a vertical image.*
- Cut 2: 1 1/2" x 8 1/2" strips, first contrasting print
- Cut 2: 1 1/2" x 5 1/2" strips, first contrasting print
- Cut 2: 1 1/2" x 5 1/2" strips, second contrasting print
- Cut 2: 1 1/2" x 3 1/2" strips, second contrasting print
- Cut 2: 1 1/2" x 5 1/2" strips, third contrasting print
- Cut 2: 1 1/2" x 3 1/2" strips, third contrasting print

Also:
- Cut 4: 1 1/2" x 46" lengthwise strips, teal print
- Cut 3: 1 1/2" x 32 1/2" strips, teal print
- Cut 8: 1 1/2" x 10 1/2" strips, teal print
- Cut 4: 2 1/2" x 44" strips, teal print, for the binding

DIRECTIONS
For each block:
- Stitch the 1 1/2" x 8 1/2" first contrasting print strips to the long sides of the 3 1/2" x 8 1/2" jungle print rectangle.
- Stitch the 1 1/2" x 5 1/2" first contrasting print strips to the remaining sides of the rectangle to complete a rectangular unit. Set it aside.
- Stitch the 1 1/2" x 3 1/2" second contrasting print strips to 2 opposite sides of a 3 1/2" jungle print square.
- Stitch the 1 1/2" x 5 1/2" second contrasting print strips to the remaining sides of the square to complete a square unit. Make 2, using the third contrasting prints for the second square unit.
- Lay out the rectangular unit and 2 square units so that they form a square, placing the rectangular unit either horizontally at the top or the bottom or vertically on the right or the left, depending on the orientation of the jungle image.
- Stitch the square units together and then stitch them to the rectangular unit to complete a block. Make 12.

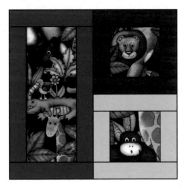 

- Lay out the blocks in 4 rows of 3, with 1 1/2" x 10 1/2" teal print strips between the blocks, and 1 1/2" x 32 1/2" teal print strips between the rows.
- Stitch the blocks and short teal print strips into rows. Join the rows and the long teal print strips.
- Measure the length of the quilt. Trim 2 of the 1 1/2" x 46" teal print strips to that measurement and stitch them to the sides of the quilt.
- Measure the width of the quilt, including the borders. Trim the remaining 1 1/2" x 46" teal print strips to that measurement and stitch them to the top and bottom of the quilt.
- Finish the quilt as described in the *General Directions*, using the 2 1/2" x 44" teal print strips for the binding.

The call of the wild is reflected in this quilt Christiane made with its jungle critter prints. **"Playmate Come Out and Play with Me"** *(34" x 45") will allow a young tot to go on a delightful imagination safari.*

Twinkle, Twinkle, Little Star

Bright colors carry this traditional block to the space age and beyond.

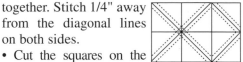

Materials

All of the solid fabrics used in the quilt are mottled.

- 1 3/4 yards white print
- 1/4 yard purple
- 1/4 yard yellow
- 5/8 yard green
- 1/4 yard pink
- 1/4 yard blue
- 1 1/2 yards backing fabric
- 36" x 46" piece of batting

QUILT SIZE: 32" x 42"
BLOCK SIZE: 6" square

CUTTING

Dimensions include a 1/4" seam allowance.
- Cut 1: 6" x 9" rectangle, from each of the 5 colors
- Cut 3: 2 1/2" squares, from each of the 5 colors
- Cut 1: 1 1/2" x 23" strip, from each of the 5 colors
- Cut 5: 6" x 9" rectangles, white print
- Cut 60: 2 1/2" squares, white print
- Cut 5: 1 1/2" x 23" strips, white print
- Cut 3: 6 1/2" squares, white print
- Cut 12: 4 1/2" x 6 1/2" rectangles, white print
- Cut 2: 1 1/2" x 38" strips, white print
- Cut 2: 1 1/2" x 30" strips, white print
- Cut 2: 1 1/2" x 42" strips, white print
- Cut 2: 1 1/2" x 35" strips, white print
- Cut 4: 2 1/2" x 44" strips, green, for the binding

DIRECTIONS

- Draw a grid of six 3" squares on the wrong side of each 6" x 9" white print rectangle. Draw diagonal lines through the centers of the squares, as shown.
- Place a marked white print rectangle on the 6" x 9" purple rectangle, right sides

together. Stitch 1/4" away from the diagonal lines on both sides.

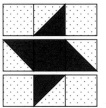

- Cut the squares on the drawn lines to yield 12 pieced squares. Press the seam allowances toward the purple. Trim the squares to 2 1/2".
- Lay out 4 pieced squares, a 2 1/2" purple square, and four 2 1/2" white print squares, as shown.

- Stitch the squares into rows and join the rows to complete a block. Make 3 blocks from each of the 5 colors, for a total of 15 blocks.
- Referring to the assembly diagram, lay out the blocks, 4 1/2" x 6 1/2" white print rectangles, and 6 1/2" white print squares in 6 rows.
- Stitch the blocks, rectangles, and squares into rows and join the rows.
- Measure the length of the quilt. Trim the 1 1/2" x 38" white print strips to that measurement and stitch them to the long sides of the quilt.
- Measure the width of the quilt, including the borders. Trim the 1 1/2" x 30" white print strips to that measurement and stitch them to the remaining sides of the quilt.

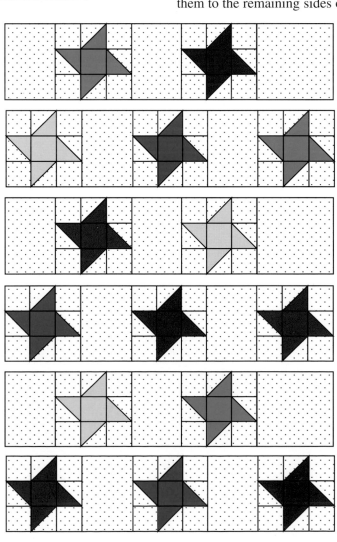

Karen stitched the sparkle in this sweet **"Twinkle, Twinkle, Little Star"** *(32" x 42") quilt. Your children can take their pick upon which of the 15 stars to hang their wishes.*

• Stitch each of the 1 1/2" x 23" colored strips to a 1 1/2" x 23" white print strip, along their length.
• Cut sixty-eight 1 1/2" slices from the pieced strips.

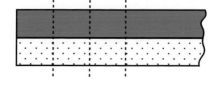

• Stitch 19 slices together alternating the colored squares with the white print squares to make a border. Make 2.
• Stitch them to the long sides of the quilt. Adjust a few seams, if necessary, to make your border fit the quilt.
• In the same manner, stitch 15 slices together to make a border. Make 2. Stitch them to the remaining sides of the quilt.
• Measure the length of the quilt. Trim the 1 1/2" x 42" white print strips to that mea-

surement and stitch them to the long sides of the quilt.
• Measure the width of the quilt, including the borders. Trim the 1 1/2" x 35" white print strips to that measurement and stitch them to the remaining sides of the quilt.
• Finish the quilt as described in the *General Directions,* using the 2 1/2" x 44" green strips for the binding.

Old McDonald Had a Farm

Bright colors and cute creatures always fascinate children.

Materials

The yardage for the animal print includes extra to allow for fussy-cutting the images. The remaining fabrics used in the quilt are mottled.

- 1 yard animal print
- 1/4 yard each of dark purple, dark pink, medium blue, dark blue, gold, orange, green, and red
- 1/8 yard medium blue
- 5/8 yard dark blue
- 1 1/2 yards backing fabric
- 38" x 46" piece of batting
- Template plastic

QUILT SIZE: 34" x 42"
BLOCK SIZE: 8" square

CUTTING

Dimensions include a 1/4" seam allowance. Make a 6" square see-through plastic template, and center animal motifs in the template when cutting fabric pieces.

- Cut 12: 6" squares, animal print
- Cut 1: 3" x 24 1/2" strip, orange
- Cut 1: 3" x 35" strip, dark purple
- Cut 1: 3" x 27" strip, dark pink
- Cut 1: 3" x 37 1/2" strip, gold
- Cut 1: 3" x 29 1/2" strip, red
- Cut 1: 3" x 40" strip, dark blue
- Cut 1: 3" x 32" strip, dark blue
- Cut 1: 3" x 42 1/2" strip, green
- Cut 12: 3" x 8 1/2" strips, assorted prints
- Cut 12: 3" x 6" strips, assorted prints
- Cut 4: 2 1/2" x 44" strips, dark blue, for the binding

DIRECTIONS

- Stitch a 3" x 6" assorted print strip to the right edge of a 6" animal print square. Press the seam allowance toward the strip.

- Stitch a 3" x 8 1/2" different print strip to the top of the animal print square, press as before, to complete Block A. Make 8.

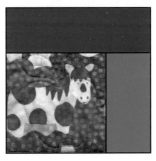

- In the same manner, stitch a 3" x 6" print strip to the right edge of a 6" animal print square.
- Stitch a 3" x 8 1/2" different print strip to the bottom of the animal print square to complete Block B. Make 4.

- Referring to the quilt photo, lay out the Block A's in 2 vertical rows with a vertical row of Block B's between them. Stitch the blocks into rows and join the rows.
- Stitch the 3" x 24 1/2" orange strip to the bottom of the quilt.
- Stitch the 3" x 35" dark purple strip to the right side of the quilt.
- Turning the quilt in the same direction, continue sewing the remaining strips to the quilt in this order: 3" x 35" dark pink, 3" x 37 1/2" gold, 3" x 29 1/2" red, 3" x 40" dark blue, 3" x 32" dark blue, and 3" x 42 1/2" green. There will be 2 strips on each side of the quilt.
- Finish the quilt as described in the *General Directions*, using the 2 1/2" x 44" dark blue strips for the binding.

"Old MacDonald Had a Farm" *(34" x 42") presents a creative way to display a juvenile print. Use lively colors for the frames like Christiane did. Your child will love it!*

You Are My Sunshine

Use strip-pieced blocks to form a brightly colored maze.

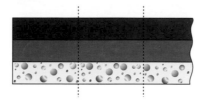

Materials

- 2 yards yellow print
- 3/8 yard red
- 3/8 yard blue
- 3/8 yard green
- 3/4 yard navy
- 2 3/4 yards backing fabric
- 46" x 60" piece of batting

QUILT SIZE: 42" x 55 1/2"
BLOCK SIZE: 4 1/2" square

CUTTING

Dimensions include a 1/4" seam allowance. Cut the lengthwise yellow print border strips before cutting smaller pieces from that fabric.

- Cut 4: 3 1/2" x 52" lengthwise strips, yellow print
- Cut 9: 2" x 44" lengthwise strips, yellow print
- Cut 4: 5" squares, yellow print
- Cut 4: 5" x 9 1/2" rectangles, yellow print
- Cut 2: 5" x 18 1/2" rectangles, yellow print
- Cut 5: 2" x 44" strips, red
- Cut 4: 2" x 44" strips, green
- Cut 4: 2" x 44" strips, blue
- Cut 5: 2" x 44" strips, navy
- Cut 6: 2 1/2" x 44" strips, navy, for the binding

DIRECTIONS

- Stitch a 2" x 44" red strip between a 2" x 44" yellow print strip and a 2" x 44" navy strip, along their length, to make a panel. Make 5.

- Cut forty 5" slices from the panels. Set them aside.

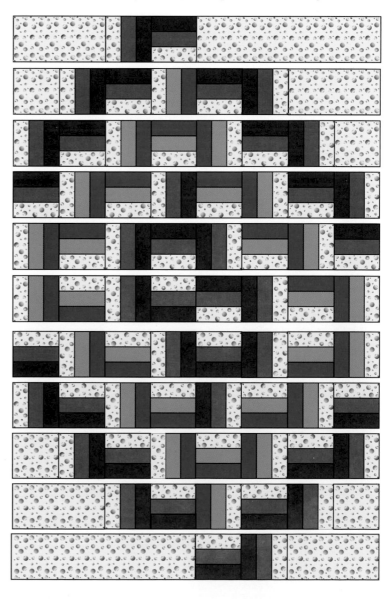

- In the same manner, stitch a 2" x 44" green strip between a 2" x 44" yellow print strip and a 2" x 44" blue strip, to make a panel. Make 4.
- Cut twenty-eight 5" slices from the panels.
- Referring to the assembly diagram, lay out the slices, the yellow print squares, and the yellow print rectangles in 11 rows. Stitch them into rows and join the rows.
- Measure the length of the quilt. Trim 2 of the 3 1/2" x 52" yellow print strips to that measurement and stitch them to the long sides of the quilt.
- Measure the width of the quilt, including the borders. Trim the remaining 3 1/2" x 52" yellow print strips to that measurement and stitch them to the remaining sides of the quilt.
- Finish the quilt according to the *General Directions,* using the 2 1/2" x 44" navy strips for the binding.

Warm up your child's room with this cheerful quilt made by Karen. **"You Are My Sunshine"** *(42" x 55 1/2") is sure to be a favorite "blankie" for a special little tyke.*

I See the Moon and the Moon Sees Me

Bright, abstract designs entertain both children and adults!

Materials

All of the solid fabrics used in the quilt are mottled.

- 1/2 yard red
- 1/2 yard blue
- 1/8 yard yellow
- 1/8 yard green
- 1/8 yard each of polka dot fabric in red, blue, yellow, light green, and dark green (NOTE: *Karen used a red check instead of a red polka dot.*)
- 1/3 yard black polka dot fabric for the binding
- 1 1/4 yards of backing fabric
- 36" x 43" piece of batting
- Template plastic

QUILT SIZE: 32" x 38 1/2"
BLOCK SIZE: 6 1/2" square

CUTTING

Pattern pieces on page 29 are full size and include a 1/4" seam allowance, as do all dimensions given. Make a template of each pattern piece. When making template B, include the diagonal line, which will be used for alignment when making some of the blocks.

- Cut 4: A, each of the five polka dot fabrics
- Cut 2: B, red
- Cut 2: 7 3/8" squares, red
- Cut 2: 3 1/2" x 35" strips, red
- Cut 3: B, yellow
- Cut 3: 7 3/8" squares, yellow
- Cut 3: B, green
- Cut 3: 7 3/8" squares, green
- Cut 2: B, blue
- Cut 2: 7 3/8" squares, blue
- Cut 2: 3 1/2" x 35" strips, blue
- Cut 4: 2 1/2" x 44" strips, black polka dot, for the binding

DIRECTIONS

- Stitch a polka dot A to a contrasting B along their curved edges to complete a block. Make 10. Set them aside.

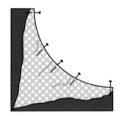

- Draw a diagonal line from corner to corner on the wrong side of the 7 3/8" yellow squares and the 7 3/8" red squares.
- Lay a marked yellow square on a 7 3/8" green square, right sides together, and stitch 1/4" away from the diagonal line on both sides, as shown.
- Cut the square on the marked line to yield 2 green/yellow pieced squares.

- In the same manner, make 4 blue/yellow pieced squares and 4 red/green pieced squares.
- Place the B template on a pieced square, aligning the diagonal seam with the diagonal line on the template. Trace around the template and cut the pieced B out along the traced line. Make 10.

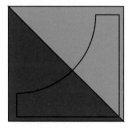

- In the same manner as before, stitch a contrasting polka dot A to a pieced B along their curved edges to complete a block. Make 10.
- Referring to the quilt photo, lay out the blocks in 5 rows of 4. Stitch the blocks into rows and join the rows.
- Measure the length of the quilt. Trim a 3 1/2" x 35" red strip and a 3 1/2" x 35" blue strip to that measurement and stitch them to the long sides of the quilt.
- Measure the width of the quilt, including the borders. Trim the remaining 3 1/2" x 35" red strip and 3 1/2" x 35" blue strip to that measurement and stitch them to the remaining sides of the quilt.
- Finish the quilt as described in the *General Directions*, using the 2 1/2" x 44" black polka dot strips for the binding.

"I See the Moon and the Moon Sees Me" *(32" x 38 1/2") will certainly give a young child lots to look at with its bright primary colors and creative shapes. Karen machine pieced the curves in this quilt, but for an even easier technique, follow the Instructions in "Fusible Web Method" below.*

Fusible Web Method

For an even quicker quilt, fuse A pieces to squares rather than piecing the blocks.

ADDITIONAL MATERIALS
• Fusible web

CUTTING
Make a template of the A pattern keeping the seam allowance along the straight sides, but eliminating it along the curved side. Trace the template 20 times on the paper side of the fusible web. Rough cut around the shapes. Following the manufacturer's directions, fuse the web to the wrong side of the polka dot fabrics making 4 A's from each of the 5 polka dot prints. Cut them out on the drawn lines. Do not use pattern piece B, but instead:
• Cut 2: 7" squares, red
• Cut 3: 7" squares, yellow
• Cut 3: 7" squares, green
• Cut 2: 7" squares, blue

DIRECTIONS
• Align the straight edges of an A with the edges of a 7" contrasting square, right sides up. Following the manufacturer's directions, fuse the A to the square. Use a finishing stitch on the curved edge to complete a block. Make 10. Set them aside.
• Refer to the main directions to make 10 pieced squares.
• Align the straight edges of an A with the edges of a pieced square, as shown.

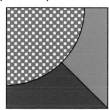

• Following the manufacturer's directions, fuse the A to the pieced square and use a finishing stitch on the curved edge to complete a block. Make 10.
• Refer to the main directions to complete the quilt.

Here We Go 'round the Mulberry Bush

Fussy-cut an exuberant stripe for maximum impact with minimum work.

Materials

- 1 yard multi-colored wide stripe
- 1/4 yard pink floral
- 1/2 yard blue floral
- 1 yard mottled blue
- 1/2 yard green print
- 1 yard yellow print
- 3/8 yard yellow stripe
- 1 1/2 yards mottled dark pink
- 1 3/4 yards backing fabric
- 42" x 54" piece of batting
- Template plastic

QUILT SIZE: 38" x 50"

CUTTING

The pattern piece on page 30 is full size and includes a 1/4" seam allowance, as do all dimensions given. Make a template of the pattern piece and use it to cut the first striped piece. Then mark the template along the edge of each stripe, and use these lines to align the template when cutting matching pieces. Make a second template of the pattern piece, and use it in the same manner to cut the second stripe sections.

- Cut 12: triangles, first matching section of the multi-colored stripe
- Cut 10: triangles, second matching section of the multi-colored stripe
- Cut 6: triangles, pink floral
- Cut 12: triangles, blue floral
- Cut 7: triangles, green print
- Cut 5: 2 1/2" x 44" strips, mottled blue, for the binding
- Cut 11: triangles, mottled blue
- Cut 30: triangles, yellow print
- Cut 4: 1 1/2" x 27" strips, yellow stripe
- Cut 2: 1 1/2" x 35" strips, yellow stripe
- Cut 4: 3 1/2" x 46" lengthwise strips, mottled dark pink

DIRECTIONS

- Referring to the assembly diagram, lay out the triangles in 8 rows of 11. Note: *The long sides of the quilt will be uneven.*
- Stitch the triangles into rows and join the rows.
- Trim the long sides of the quilt 1/4" beyond the center point of the triangles, as shown in the assembly diagram.
- Stitch 2 of the 1 1/2" x 27" yellow stripe strips together, end to end, to make a pieced border strip. Make 2.
- Center and stitch the pieced border strips to the long sides of the quilt. Start, stop, and backstitch 1/4" from the raw edges of the quilt top.
- Center and stitch the 1 1/2" x 35" yellow stripe strips to the remaining sides of the quilt in the same manner. Miter each corner referring to the *General Directions*, as needed.
- Measure the length of the quilt. Trim 2 of the 3 1/2" x 46" mottled dark pink strips to that measurement and stitch them to the long sides of the quilt.
- Measure the width of the quilt, including the borders. Trim the remaining 3 1/2" x 46" mottled dark pink strips to that measurement and stitch them to the remaining sides of the quilt.
- Finish the quilt as described in the *General Directions,* using the 2 1/2" x 44" mottled blue strips for the binding.

"Here We Go 'round the Mulberry Bush" *(38" x 50")* *was stitched by Karen. This dynamic quilt looks complicated, but it's not. The secret is to use an interesting striped fabric to form the center of the wheel.*

Do You Believe in Magic?

Display your tot's favorite character in this triangular design.

Materials

The red and blue solid fabrics used in this quilt are mottled.

- 1 yard juvenile print
- 1 1/2 yards red
- 1/2 yard blue
- 1/2 yard gold print
- 1 1/2 yards dark blue print
- 1 1/2 yards light blue print
- 1/2 yard navy for the binding
- 1 1/2 yards backing fabric

NOTE: *If fabric is less than 42" wide, you will need 2 1/4 yards.*

- 43" x 54" piece of batting
- Template plastic

QUILT SIZE: 38 1/2" x 49 1/2"

CUTTING

The pattern piece on page 30 is full size and includes a 1/4" seam allowance, as do all dimensions given. Make a see-through plastic template of the pattern piece, and center motif in the template when cutting fabric pieces, as desired. Cut the lengthwise strips before cutting smaller pieces from those fabrics.

- Cut 24: triangles, juvenile print. NOTE: *If you are planning to fussy cut images to place in the triangles, refer to the quilt photo for orientation.*
- Cut 2: 1 1/2" x 50" lengthwise strips, red
- Cut 24: 1 3/4" x 12" strips, red
- Cut 24: 1 3/4" x 12" strips, blue
- Cut 24: 1 3/4" x 12" strips, gold print
- Cut 2: 1 1/2" x 40" strips, gold print
- Cut 2: 1" x 50" lengthwise strips, dark blue print
- Cut 2: 3 1/2" x 50" lengthwise strips, dark blue print
- Cut 2: 1" x 40" strips, dark blue print
- Cut 2: 3 1/2" x 40" strips, dark blue print
- Cut 2: 1 3/4" x 50" lengthwise strips, light blue print
- Cut 2: 1 3/4" x 40" strips, light blue print

- Cut 5: 2 1/2" x 44" strips, navy, for the binding

DIRECTIONS

- Center and stitch a 1 3/4" x 12" red strip along the right side of a juvenile print triangle. Press the seam allowance toward the strip.
- Trim the ends of the red strip even with the triangle.

- Center and stitch a 1 3/4" x 12" red strip to the left side of the triangle and press as before. Trim the ends.

- Stitch a 1 3/4" x 12" red strip to the remaining side of the triangle. Press and trim, as before, to complete a red triangle unit. Make 8 red, 8 blue, and 8 gold.

- Referring to the quilt photo, lay out the blocks in 4 rows of 6. NOTE: *The long sides of the quilt will be uneven.*
- Stitch the blocks into rows and join the rows.
- Trim the long sides of the quilt 1/4" beyond the center point of the outermost blocks, as shown.

- Stitch a 1 3/4" x 40" light blue print strip between a 1" x 40" dark blue print strip and a 1 1/2" x 40" gold print strip, along their length. Stitch a 3 1/2" x 40" dark blue print strip to the gold print edge to complete a short pieced border. Make 2. Press all seam allowances toward the wide dark blue print strip.
- In the same manner, stitch a 1 3/4" x 50" light blue print strip between a 1" x 50" dark blue print strip and a 1 1/2" x 50" red strip. Stitch a 3 1/2" x 50" dark blue print strip to the red edge to complete a long pieced border. Make 2. Press, as before.
- Pin a short border to the upper edge of the quilt, aligning it with the left edge of the quilt, and placing the narrow dark blue print against the quilt center.

"Do You Believe in Magic?" *(38 1/2" x 49 1/2") was great fun for Christiane to make. We know you will enjoy making it too! Fussy cutting a special fabric like the Harry Potter motifs used here and framing them in bright fabrics adds to the excitement.*

• Stitch a partial seam, beginning at the left edge of the quilt and stopping approximately 6" from the opposite end of the quilt top. Press the seam allowance toward the border.

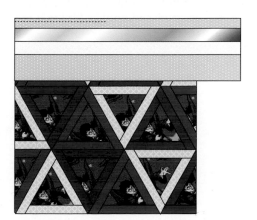

• Measure the length of the left side of the quilt, including the attached border. Trim a long pieced border to that measurement and stitch it to that side. Press as before.

• Measure the width of the quilt including the attached border and trim the remaining short pieced border to that measurement. Stitch it to the bottom of the quilt. Press as before.

• Measure the length of the right side of the quilt, including the bottom border. Trim a long pieced border to that measurement and stitch it to that side. Press as before.

• Complete the upper right corner seam. Trim the top border, as necessary.

• Finish the quilt as described in the *General Directions*, using the 2 1/2" x 44" navy strips for the binding

Knick, Knack, Paddy Whack

This quilt can be pieced in a jiffy!

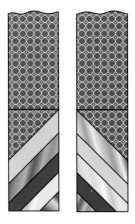

Materials

- 1/4 yard each of 6 mottled fabrics in yellow, gold, blue, green, pink, and purple
- 1 1/2 yards blue print
- 3/4 yard mottled red for the binding
- 1 1/2 yards backing fabric
- 36" x 49" piece of batting
- Template plastic

QUILT SIZE: 32" x 45"
BLOCK SIZE: 6 1/2" square

CUTTING

The pattern piece on page 31 is full size and includes a 1/4" seam allowance as do all dimensions given. Make a template of the pattern piece.

- Cut 25: 1 1/2" x 33" strips, assorted mottled fabrics
- Cut 4: 7" squares, blue print
- Cut 12: 7 3/8" squares, blue print, then cut them in half diagonally to yield 24 triangles
- Cut 4: 3 1/2" x 13 1/2" strips, blue print
- Cut 2: 3 1/2" x 34" strips, blue print
- Cut 5: 2 1/2" x 44" strips, mottled red, for the binding

DIRECTIONS

- Stitch five assorted 1 1/2" x 33" mottled strips together along their length to make a panel.
- Make 4 additional panels each with a different strip arrangement.
- Using the template, trace and cut 5 pieced triangles from each panel, as shown. You will use 24.

- Stitch a pieced triangle to a blue print triangle to complete a block. Make 24. Set 4 blocks aside.
- Lay out the blocks and the 7" blue print squares in 6 rows of 4, as shown.

- Stitch the blocks into rows. Join the rows.
- Cut 2 of the remaining blocks in half, as shown.

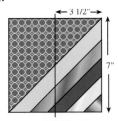

- Cut the remaining blocks in half, as shown.

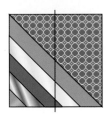

- Discard the sections with the fewest number of pieced strips.
- Stitch each remaining section to a 3 1/2" x 13 1/2" blue print strip to make a pieced section. Stitch 2 of each, as shown.

- Stitch two pieced sections together to make a pieced border, as shown. Make 2.
- Referring to the quilt photo for directional placement, stitch the pieced borders to the long sides of the quilt.
- Measure the width of the quilt, including the borders. Trim the 3 1/2" x 34" blue print strips to that measurement and stitch them to the remaining sides of the quilt.
- Finish the quilt according to the *General Directions*, using the 2 1/2" x 44" mottled red strips for the binding.

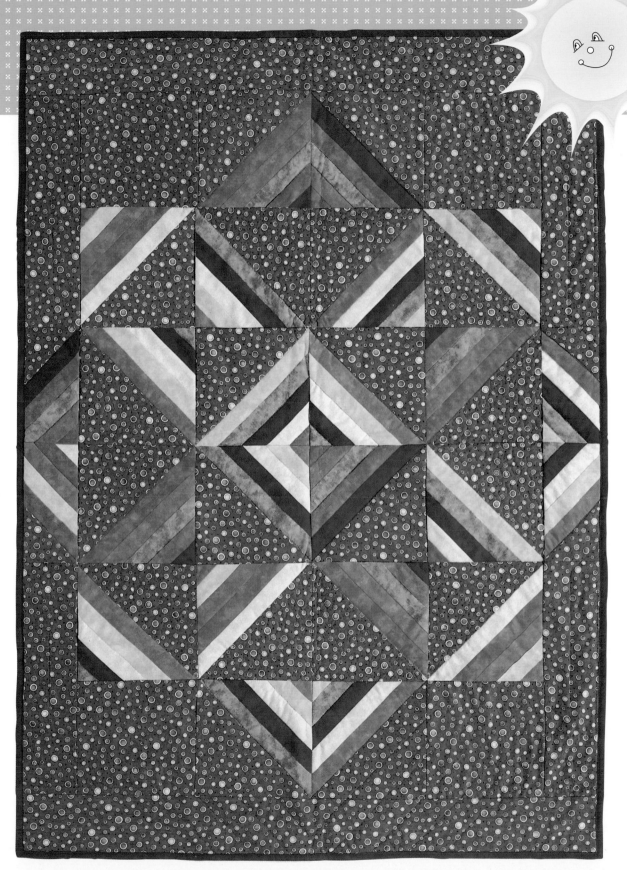

Pick an array of your favorite colors for **"Knick, Knack, Paddy Whack"** *(32" x 45"). Karen's radiant quilt will nicely brighten the nursery or playroom of a special toddler.*

Ring Around the Rosie

Corral a herd of mythic animals with brightly colored "fences."

The yardage for the unicorn print includes extra to allow for fussy-cutting the images. All of the solid fabrics used in the quilt are mottled.

- 1 yard pink unicorn print
- 1/8 yard purple
- 1/8 yard green
- 1/8 yard light blue
- 1/8 yard teal
- 1/8 yard dark pink
- 1 yard purple print
- 1 1/2 yards backing fabric
- 39" x 47" piece of batting
- Template plastic

QUILT SIZE: 34 1/2" x 42 1/2"
BLOCK SIZE: 5 1/2" square

CUTTING

Dimensions include a 1/4" seam allowance. Make a 3" and a 6" square see-through plastic template, and center motifs in the template when cutting fabric pieces.

- Cut 12: 6" squares, pink unicorn print
- Cut 20: 3" squares, pink unicorn print
- Cut 31: 3" x 6" strips, assorted solids
- Cut 4: 4 1/2" x 37" strips, purple print
- Cut 4: 2 1/2" x 44" strips, purple print, for the binding

DIRECTIONS

• Lay out three 6" pink unicorn print squares with 3" x 6" assorted strips between them and at the beginning and end. Stitch them together to complete a row. Make 4.

• Lay out four 3" pink unicorn print squares with 3" x 6" assorted strips between them. Stitch them together to complete a sashing. Make 5.

• Lay out the sashings alternately with the rows. Stitch them together.
• Measure the length of the quilt. Trim 2 of the 4 1/2" x 37" purple print strips to that measurement and stitch them to the long sides of the quilt.
• Measure the width of the quilt, including the borders. Trim the remaining 4 1/2" x 37" purple print strips to that measurement and stitch them to the top and bottom of the quilt.
• Finish the quilt as described in the *General Directions,* using the 2 1/2" x 44" purple print strips for the binding.

Your youngster will think she is in fantasy land when you make her a **"Ring Around the Rosie"** (34 1/2" x 42 1/2") quilt. "I'm certain pretty unicorns framed in mottled pastels will inspire hours of playing pretend," says quiltmaker Christiane.

How Much is that Doggie in the Window?

Use soft flannels to create this cute litter of puppies.

Materials

The fabrics used in the quilt are flannel. The yardage for the puppy print includes extra to allow for fussy-cutting the image. We recommend pre-washing and machine drying flannel.

- 1/2 yard puppy print
- 1/2 yard blue
- 1 yard red
- 1/2 yard yellow
- 1/2 yard mottled green
- 1 1/2 yards tan plaid
- 1 1/4 yards backing fabric
- 43" piece of batting
- Template plastic

QUILT SIZE: 38 1/2" square
BLOCK SIZE: 6" square

CUTTING

Dimensions include a 1/4" seam allowance. Make a 4" square see-through plastic template, and center a puppy motif in the template when cutting fabric pieces.

- Cut 20: 4" squares, puppy print
- Cut 20: 1 3/4" x 5 1/4" strips, blue
- Cut 1: 1 3/4" x 32" strip, blue
- Cut 1: 5 1/4" x 8" strip, blue
- Cut 5: 2 1/2" x 44" strips, red, for the binding
- Cut 20: 1 3/4" x 5 1/4" strips, red
- Cut 1: 1 3/4" x 32" strip, red
- Cut 1: 1 3/4" x 10" strip, red
- Cut 20: 1 3/4" x 5 1/4" strips, yellow
- Cut 1: 1 3/4" x 32" strip, yellow
- Cut 20: 1 3/4" x 5 1/4" strips, mottled green
- Cut 1: 5 1/4" x 10" strip, mottled green
- Cut 1: 1 3/4" x 8" strip, mottled green
- Cut 1: 1 3/4" square, mottled green
- Cut 3: 5 1/4" x 32" strips, tan plaid
- Cut 2: 3 1/2" x 7 3/4" rectangles, tan plaid
- Cut 7: 3 1/2" x 6 1/2" rectangles, tan plaid
- Cut 1: 1 3/4" x 6 1/2" strip, tan plaid
- Cut 2: 1 1/2" x 6 1/2" strips, tan plaid

DIRECTIONS

- Stitch a 1 3/4" x 5 1/4" blue strip to the top of a 4" puppy print square, starting at the left edge and stopping at least 1" from the end of the square, as shown.

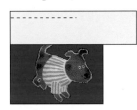

- Open the unit and press the seam allowance toward the strip.
- Stitch a 1 3/4" x 5 1/4" mottled green strip the left side of the puppy print square and press, as before.

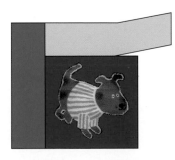

- Stitch a 1 3/4" x 5 1/4" red strip to the bottom and a 1 3/4" x 5 1/4" yellow strip to the right side in the same manner.
- Complete the first seam by stitching the remainder of the blue strip to the top of the puppy print square and to the yellow strip to complete a block. Make 20.

- Lay out the blocks in 5 rows of 4. Stitch the blocks into rows and join the rows.
- Stitch a 5 1/4" x 8" blue strip to a 1 3/4" x 8" mottled green strip, along their length.
- Cut four 1 3/4" sections from the pieced strip.

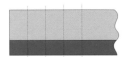

- Stitch the sections together, green end to blue end to form a row. Stitch it to the bottom of the quilt so that the mottled green squares line up with the green strips in the blocks, as shown in the assembly diagram on page 25.
- Stitch a 1 3/4" x 32" yellow strip to a 5 1/4" x 32" tan plaid strip, along their length. Cut six 3 1/2" sections and two 2 1/2" sections from the pieced strip.
- Stitch four 3 1/2" sections together to form a short pieced border.
- Stitch it to the top of the quilt so that the yellow strips in the border line up with the yellow strips in the blocks.
- Stitch a 1 1/2" x 6 1/2" tan plaid strip to each of the two 2 1/2" sections, as shown.

- Lay them out alternately with the 2 remaining 3 1/2" sections, and stitch them together to form a short pieced border.

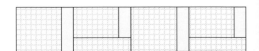

- Stitch it to the bottom of the quilt so that the yellow strips line up, as before.
- Stitch a 5 1/4" x 10" mottled green strip to a 1 3/4" x 10" red strip, along their

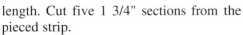

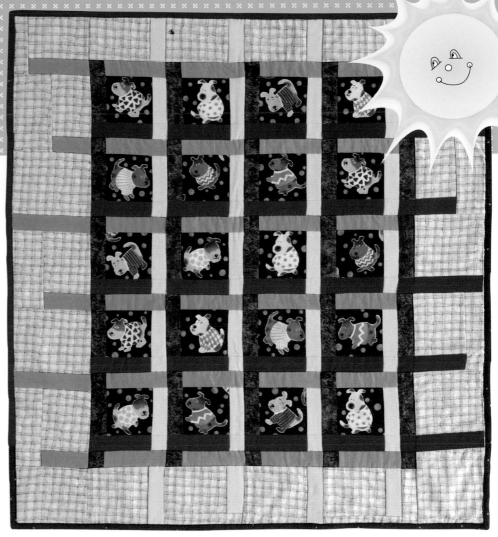

length. Cut five 1 3/4" sections from the pieced strip.

• Stitch the sections together, end to end. Stitch a 1 3/4" mottled green square to the red end to complete a pieced inner border. Set it aside.

• Stitch a 1 3/4" x 32" red strip to a 5 1/4" x 32" tan plaid strip, along their length. Cut three 6 1/2" sections and two 3 1/2" sections from the pieced strip.

• In the same manner as before, stitch a 3 1/2" x 6 1/2" tan plaid rectangle to each of the 3 1/2" sections.

• Lay them out alternately with the 6 1/2" sections, as shown, and stitch them together. Stitch a 1 3/4" x 6 1/2" plaid strip to the red end.

• Stitch the border to the green and red inner pieced border, as shown in the assembly diagram.

• Stitch a 3 1/2" x 7 3/4" tan plaid rectangle to each end. Stitch the border to the right side of the quilt.

• Stitch a 1 3/4" x 32" blue strip to a 5 1/4" x 32" tan plaid strip, along their length. Cut three 6 1/2" sections and three 3 1/2" sections from the pieced strip.

• Stitch a 3 1/2" x 6 1/2" tan plaid rectangle to each of the 3 1/2" sections.

• Lay them out alternately with the 6 1/2" sections, as shown in the assembly diagram, and stitch them together. Stitch 3 1/2" x 6 1/2" tan plaid rectangles to the ends.

• Stitch it to the left side of the quilt.

• Finish the quilt as described in the *General Directions*, using the 2 1/2" x 44" red strips for the binding.

"How Much is that Doggie in the Window?" *(38 1/2" square) was pieced by Karen who used flannels so that the quilt would be as soft as a puppy! Won't your tot enjoy counting all the puppies!*

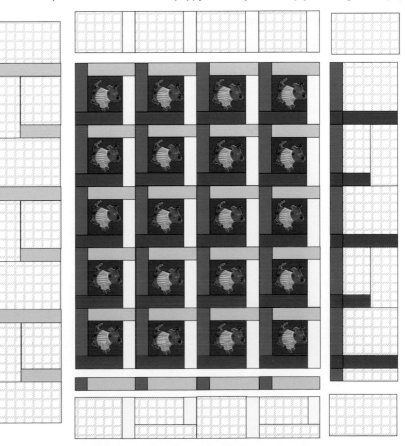

If You're Happy and You Know It

Stitch a quick quilt for those little smiling faces in your life.

Materials

- 3/4 yard navy print
- 1/2 yard red print
- 1/2 yard gold print
- 1 yard mottled green
- 1 1/4 yards backing fabric
- 36" x 44" piece of batting

QUILT SIZE: 31 1/4" x 39 1/2"
BLOCK SIZE: 6 3/4" square

CUTTING

Dimensions include a 1/4" seam allowance.
- Cut 4: 3" x 32" strips, navy print
- Cut 4: 2 1/2" x 44" strips, navy print, for the binding
- Cut 4: 3" x 32" strips, red print
- Cut 4: 3" x 32" strips, gold print
- Cut 8: 2" x 7 1/4" strips, mottled green
- Cut 3: 2" x 23 3/4" strips, mottled green
- Cut 4: 4 1/2" x 34" strips, mottled green

DIRECTIONS

- Stitch a 3" x 32" red print strip between a 3" x 32" navy print strip and a 3" x 32" gold print strip, along their length, to make a pieced strip. Make 4.
- Press the seam allowances in one direction on 2 of the pieced strips and in the opposite direction on the remaining pieced strips.
- Cut three 8" sections and one 5 1/2" section from each pieced strip.

- Draw a diagonal line from corner to corner on the wrong side of six 8" sections with their seams pressed in the same direction.

- Lay a marked 8" section on an unmarked 8" section, right sides together, with the prints in the top section aligned with the same prints in the bottom section. Pin at the seamlines. Stitch 1/4" away from the diagonal line on both sides. Make 6.

- Cut the squares on the marked line to yield 6 of each block, as shown.

- Trim the blocks to 7 1/4" square.

- Referring to the quilt photo, lay out the blocks in 4 rows of 3.
- Place the 2" x 7 1/4" mottled green strips between the blocks in each horizontal row. Join the blocks and strips in each row.

- Place the 2" x 23 3/4" mottled green strips between the rows and stitch the strips and rows together.
- Remove the gold print strip from each of the four 5 1/2" slices previously cut from the pieced strips.
- Draw a diagonal line from corner to corner on the wrong side of 2 sections with their seams pressed in the same direction.
- Lay a marked section on an unmarked section, right sides together, and with the prints in the top section aligned with the same prints in the bottom section. Pin and then stitch 1/4" away from the diagonal line on both sides. Cut the squares on the marked lines to yield 2 border blocks, as shown. Repeat with the remaining sections.

- Trim the blocks to 4 1/2" square.
- Measure the width of the quilt. Trim 2 of the 4 1/2" x 34" mottled green strips to that measurement. Referring to the photo, stitch border blocks to the ends of each strip. Set them aside.
- Measure the length of the quilt. Trim the remaining 4 1/2" x 34" mottled green strips to that measurement. Stitch them to the long sides of the quilt.
- Stitch the pieced borders to the short sides of the quilt.
- Finish the quilt as described in the *General Directions,* using the 2 1/2" x 44" navy print strips for the binding.

Christiane used vivid fabrics to create **"If You're Happy and You Know It"** (31 1/4" x 391/2"). With its cheerful colors, this lively quilt is sure to delight every youngster.

EASIER METHOD

While the diagonal seams in the main directions are simple, alignment of the seams can be intimidating to some quilters. Here is an alternative cutting and stitching method with a similar finished appearance.

CUTTING

Dimensions include a 1/4" seam allowance.

- Cut 6: 2 1/2" squares, gold print
- Cut 6: 2 3/4" x 5" strips, gold print
- Cut 6: 2 3/4" x 7 1/4" strips, gold print
- Cut 12: 2 1/2" x 3" rectangles, red print
- Cut 12: 3" x 5" rectangles, red print
- Cut 4: 2 1/2" squares, red print
- Cut 2: 2 1/2" x 4 1/2" strips, red print
- Cut 10: 2 1/2" squares, navy print
- Cut 6: 2 3/4" x 5" strips, navy print
- Cut 6: 2 3/4" x 7 1/4" strips, navy print
- Cut 2: 2 1/2" x 4 1/2" strips, navy print
- Cut 8: 2" x 7 1/4" strips, mottled green
- Cut 3: 2" x 23 3/4" strips, mottled green
- Cut 4: 4 1/2" x 34" strips, mottled green
- Cut 4: 2 1/2" x 44" strips, navy print, for the binding

DIRECTIONS

- Stitch a 2 1/2" x 3" red print rectangle to a 2 1/2" gold print square. Press the seam allowance toward the red print.
- Stitch a 3" x 5" red print rectangle to the adjacent side of the gold print square, and press as before.

- Stitch a 2 3/4" x 5" navy print strip to the top of the unit, and then stitch a 2 3/4" x 7 1/4" navy print strip to the right side of the unit to complete a block. Make 6.
- Make 6 more blocks reversing the placement of the gold and navy prints.
- Refer to the main directions to lay out and join the blocks.

For the border blocks:

- Stitch a 2 1/2" navy print square to a 2 1/2" red print square. Make 4.
- Stitch a 2 1/2" x 4 1/2" navy print strip to 2 of these units and a 2 1/2" x 4 1/2" red print stip to the remaining units to complete the 4 border blocks.
- Refer to the main directions for trimming, piecing, and attaching the borders.

Rock-a-bye-Baby

This flannel lullaby will lead the way to sweet dreams.

Materials

The fabrics used in the quilt are flannel. We recommend pre-washing and machine drying flannel.

- 1 3/4 yards blue print
- 3/4 yard white
- 1 1/4 yards backing fabric
- 37" x 43" piece of batting

QUILT SIZE: 33" x 39"
BLOCK SIZE: 3" square

CUTTING

Dimensions include a 1/4" seam allowance.
- Cut 8: 8" squares, white
- Cut 8: 5" squares, white
- Cut 4: 2 1/2" x 44" strips, blue print, for the binding
- Cut 4: 5" x 36" strips, blue print
- Cut 8: 8" squares, blue print
- Cut 8: 5" squares, blue print

DIRECTIONS

- Draw diagonal lines from corner to corner on the wrong side of each 5" white square. Draw horizontal and vertical lines through the centers.
- Place a marked white square on a 5" blue print square, right sides together. Stitch 1/4" away from the diagonal lines on both sides. Make 8.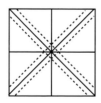
- Cut the squares on the drawn lines to yield 64 pieced squares. Press the seam allowances toward the blue print. Trim the pieced squares to 2" square.
- Lay out 4 pieced squares, as shown. Stitch them into pairs and join the pairs to complete a Pinwheel Block. Make 16. Set them aside.

"Rock-a-bye-Baby" *(33" x 39") is a soft and warm way to snuggle your toddler on cool nights. Christiane selected a cute novelty flannel to use in this quilt.*

- In the same manner, use the 8" white and 8" blue print squares to make 64 pieced squares, and trim them to 3 1/2" square.
- Referring to the quilt photo, lay out the pieced squares and Pinwheel Blocks in 10 rows of 8. Stitch the squares and blocks into rows and join the rows.
- Measure the length of the quilt. Trim 2 of the 5" x 36" blue print strips to that measurement and stitch them to the long sides of the quilt.
- Measure the width of the quilt, including the borders. Trim the remaining 5" x 36" blue print strips to that measurement and stitch them to the remaining sides of the quilt.
- Finish the quilt as described in the *General Directions,* using the 2 1/2" x 44" blue print strips for the binding.

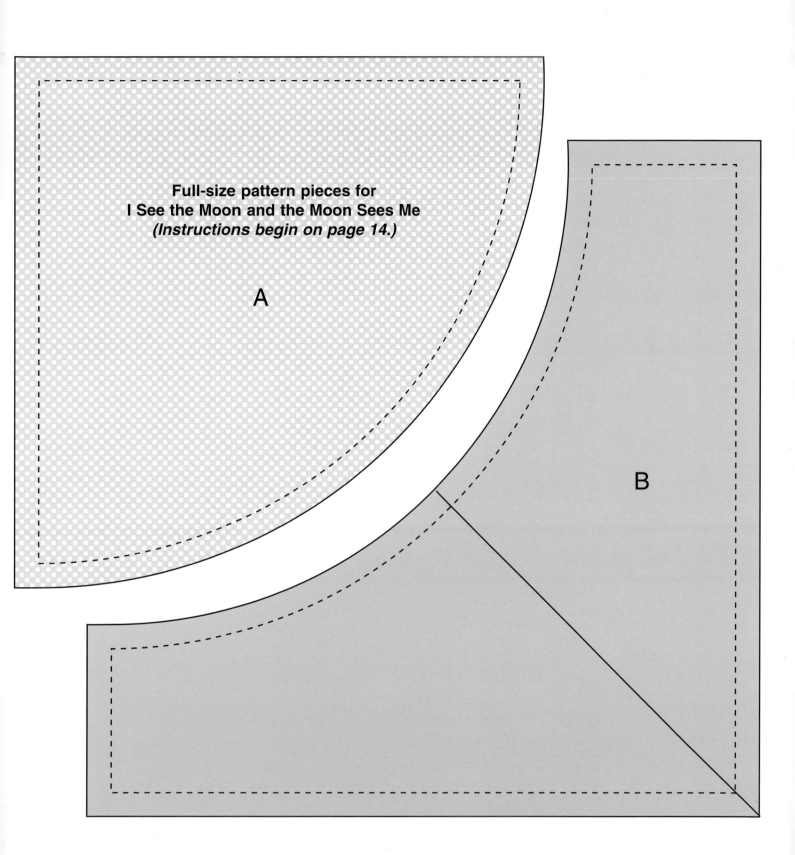

**Full-size pattern pieces for
I See the Moon and the Moon Sees Me**
(Instructions begin on page 14.)

A

B

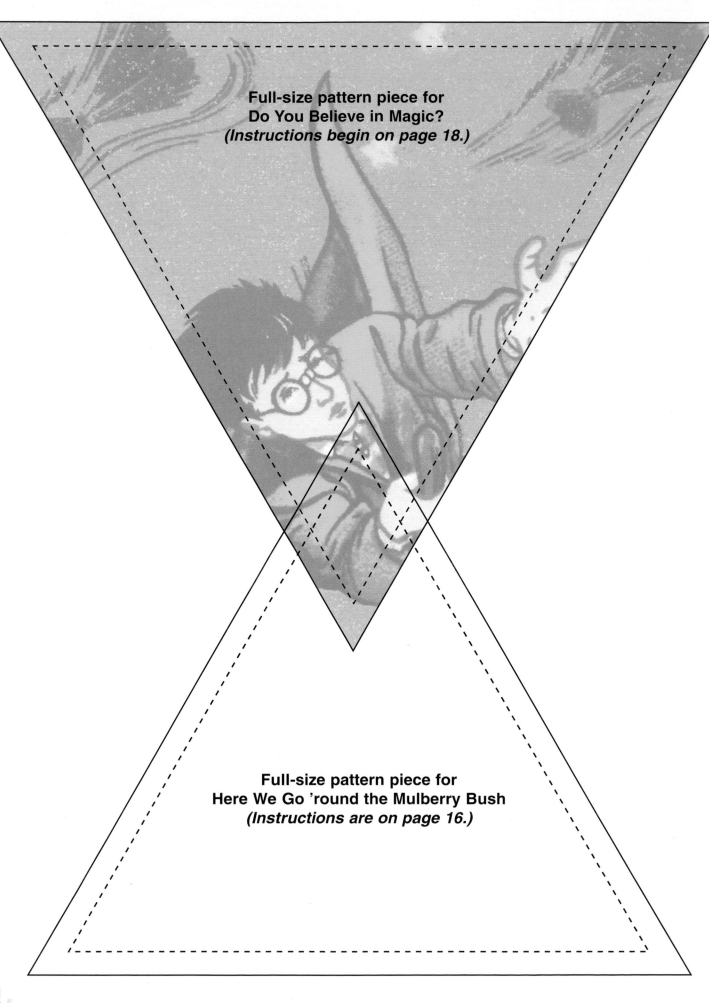

**Full-size pattern piece for
Do You Believe in Magic?**
(Instructions begin on page 18.)

**Full-size pattern piece for
Here We Go 'round the Mulberry Bush**
(Instructions are on page 16.)

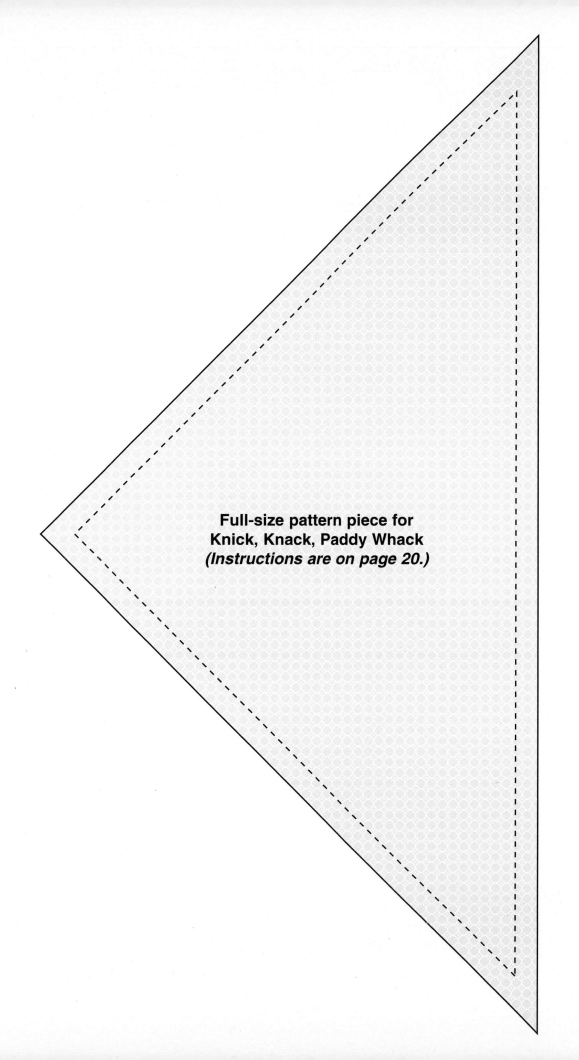

Full-size pattern piece for
Knick, Knack, Paddy Whack
(Instructions are on page 20.)

General

ABOUT THE PATTERNS

Read through the pattern directions before cutting fabric. Yardage requirements are based on 44"-wide fabric with a useable width of 42". Pattern directions are given in step-by-step order. If you are sending your quilt to a professional machine quilter, consult them regarding the necessary batting and backing size for your quilt. Batting and backing dimensions listed in the patterns are for hand quilting.

FABRICS

We suggest using 100% cotton. Wash fabric in warm water with mild detergent and no fabric softener. Dry fabric on a warm-to-hot setting. Press with a hot dry iron to remove wrinkles.

TEMPLATES

Template patterns are full size and, unless otherwise noted, include a 1/4" seam allowance. The solid line is the cutting line; the dashed line is the stitching line. Place a sheet of firm, clear plastic over the patterns and trace the cutting line and/or stitching line for each one. Templates for machine piecing include a seam allowance, templates for hand piecing generally do not.

FUSSY-CUTTING

To center fabric motifs within block pieces as in some of the quilts, make a clear plastic template of the pattern piece. Place the template on the right side of the fabric and position it so the motif is in the desired location. Trace around the template, and cut out the fabric piece on the traced line.

MARKING THE FABRIC

Test marking tools for removability before using them. Sharpen pencils often. Align the grainline on the template with the grainline of the fabric. Place a piece of fine sandpaper beneath the fabric to prevent slipping, if desired. For machine piecing, mark the right side of the fabric. For hand piecing, mark the wrong side of the fabric.

PIECING

For machine piecing, sew 12 stitches per inch, exactly 1/4" from the edge of the fabric. To make accurate piecing easier, mark the throat plate with a piece of tape 1/4" away from the point where the needle pierces the fabric. Start and stop stitching at the cut edges unless instructed to do otherwise in the pattern.

For hand piecing, begin with a small knot. Continue with a small running stitch, backstitching every 3-4 stitches. Stitch directly on the marked line from point to point, not edge to edge. Finish with two small backstitches before cutting the thread.

PRESSING

Press with a dry iron. Press seam allowances toward the darker of the two pieces whenever possible. Otherwise, trim away 1/16" from the darker seam allowance to prevent it from showing through. Press all blocks, sashings, and borders before assembling the quilt top.

FINISHING YOUR QUILT
MARKING

Mark before basting the quilt top together with the batting and backing. Chalk pencils show well on dark fabrics, otherwise use a very hard (#3 or #4) pencil or other marker for this purpose. Test your marker for removability first.

Transfer paper designs by placing fabric over the design and tracing. A light box may be necessary for darker fabrics. Precut plastic stencils that fit the area you wish to quilt may be placed on top of the quilt and traced. Use a ruler to mark straight, even grids. Masking tape can also be used to mark straight lines. Temporary quilting stencils can be made from clear adhesive-backed paper or freezer paper and reused many times. To avoid residue, do not leave tape or adhesive-backed paper on your quilt overnight.

Outline quilting does not require marking. Simply eyeball 1/4" from the seam or stitch "in the ditch" next to the seam. To prevent uneven stitching, try to avoid quilting through seam allowances wherever possible.

BASTING

Cut the batting and backing at least 4" larger than the quilt top. Tape the backing, wrong side up, on a flat surface to anchor it. Smooth the batting on top, followed by the quilt top, right side up. Baste the three layers together to form a quilt sandwich. Begin at the center and baste horizontally, then vertically. Add more lines of basting approximately every 6" until the entire top is secured.

QUILTING

Quilting is done with a short, strong needle called a "between." The lower the number (size) of the needle, the larger it is. Begin with an 8 or 9 and progress to a 10 to 12. Use a thimble on the middle finger of the hand that pushes the needle. Begin quilting at the center of the quilt and work outward to keep the tension even and the quilting smooth.

Using an 18" length of quilting thread knotted at one end, insert the needle through the quilt top only and bring it up exactly where you will begin. Pop the knot through the fabric to bury it. Push the needle straight down into the quilt with the thimbled finger of the upper hand and slightly depress the fabric in front of the needle with the thumb. Redirect the needle back to the top of the quilt using the middle or index finger of the lower hand.

Repeat with each stitch using a rocking motion. Finish by knotting the thread close to the surface and popping the knot through the fabric to bury it. Remove